Spiritual Biographies
FOR YOUNG PEOPLE

Black Elk
Native American
Man of Spirit

Maura D. Shaw • Illustrations by Stephen Marchesi

Walking Together, Finding the Way
SKYLIGHT PATHS Publishing
Woodstock, Vermont

Who Was Black Elk?

Black Elk was only a young boy when he had a dream that showed him the sacred hoop of the world, where all living things dwell together within one circle. In this vision Black Elk learned that he had a special purpose in his life: to protect his people, the Oglala Lakota Sioux of the western plains, and to pass along the knowledge of their traditional ways of life and their sacred ceremonies. His teachings of love and respect extend, as he explained, to all the two-leggeds, the four-leggeds, the wings of the air, and the green things that live on the earth.

When you learn about Black Elk's life, you will see what makes him amazing. Through the book *Black Elk Speaks*, written by his friend John Neihardt in 1931, Black Elk helped the world to understand the Plains Indians' religion and culture. Through his vision he kept the Native American way of life from disappearing.

Black Elk's friend Standing Bear painted this picture of Black Elk
with the Six Grandfathers in the flaming rainbow tipi.

Black Elk's Spirit Dream

Black Elk grew up on the plains of Wyoming at a time when his people still traveled with their tipis to hunt bison and still called the months of the year by their Indian names. When he was nine years old, in 1872, he became very sick and slept for twelve days. While he was asleep, Black Elk had a spirit dream, or vision, in which he visited the Six Grandfathers—known as the Powers of the World—who gave him special gifts of healing, seeing, and teaching.

Bison on the plains shed their shaggy winter coats each spring.

In his dream he flew up to a cloud that turned into a tipi with a flaming rainbow. He saw the sacred hoop of the world, which held all living beings in smaller hoops within it. Black Elk later said that the hoops made a circle "wide as daylight and as starlight, and in the center grew one mighty flowering tree to shelter all the children of one mother and one father."

Black Elk as a Young Warrior

At first Black Elk didn't tell anyone of his vision where he saw all living things as one family—the children of the earth created by the Great Spirit. At the age of thirteen he fought alongside his cousin Crazy Horse in the battle of the Little Bighorn to drive away the United States soldiers who were taking over the land that his people thought belonged to no one—and to everyone. But the Indian way of life was fast disappearing.

When he was about seventeen, Black Elk finally told part of his vision to a medicine man, who created a ceremony to help him follow his spiritual path as the Six Grandfathers wished. The ceremony was called the Horse Dance, which Black Elk had seen in his dream. Young women sang while braves rode horses of four different colors, representing the four directions: black horses for the west, white horses for the north, sorrel (red) horses for the east, and buckskin (yellow) horses for the south. In 1887, when he was twenty-four, Black Elk traveled across the ocean with Buffalo Bill's Wild West Show. In England, France, and Germany he performed Native American dances and showed the warrior's way of riding and shooting bareback. But Black Elk became homesick. He had another vision of his people growing hungry and sad, the sacred flowering tree becoming wilted and brown. After nearly three years Black Elk went home to the plains.

There Black Elk joined in the Ghost Dance. In the 1880s an Indian leader named Wovoka promised that dancing in a special way, called the Ghost Dance, would help the warriors drive all the soldiers away so the Indian people could live peacefully forever in their homeland. Black Elk and many others believed him. But the Ghost Dance did not protect the warriors after all. At the last tragic battle at Wounded Knee in 1890, Black Elk saw about two hundred Sioux men, women, and children killed by United States soldiers. After that battle, the Indians were forced onto reservations. Black Elk went to live on the Pine Ridge Reservation in South Dakota. He feared that the sacred hoop of the world was breaking apart.

The Beginning of *Black Elk Speaks*

Forty years after the battle of Wounded Knee, a poet named John Neihardt came to the Pine Ridge Reservation, hoping to talk with a few old men who could tell him stories of the Ghost Dance of long ago. When he drove up into the hills where Black Elk lived, he found the old man, now almost seventy years old, waiting for him in front of a broken-down log cabin. Black Elk seemed to have known that this stranger was coming.

After sitting with Neihardt in silence for a time, Black Elk said, "As I sit here I can feel in this man beside me a strong desire to know the things of the Other World. He has been sent to learn what I know, and I will teach him."

That very day Black Elk gave Neihardt a sacred ornament called the Morning Star, which Black Elk and his father, also a Native American holy man, had used in ceremonies of the Plains Indian tradition. It was a leather star, with a strip of bison hide and an eagle feather hanging from the center. The

John Neihardt *(far right)* listens to Black Elk's words
as his daughter Enid *(far left)* writes them down.

Morning Star would help the white man see wisdom, said Black Elk. The eagle feather would help his thoughts rise as high as the eagle flies, and the bison hide would bring all the good things of the earth to him. Finally, the old man began to tell the poet of his life and his dreams. John Neihardt asked whether Black Elk might allow him to publish his memories of Native American sacred traditions in a book. Black Elk agreed and invited him to return in the spring.

Standing Bear, Black Elk, and a friend
in full ceremonial dress.

Storytelling Is Hard Work

In May 1931, John Neihardt and his two daughters traveled to the reservation to live with Black Elk's family for a month. The Black Elks had a rough cabin, and the Neihardts were given a beautiful tipi painted with Lakota designs. Every day Black Elk and his best friend, Standing Bear, would sit on blankets in the shade of pine trees, telling John Neihardt the stories and traditions of the past. Black Elk spoke in the Lakota language, which his son Ben translated into English. Enid, Neihardt's older daughter, carefully wrote down every word. Neihardt asked many questions to make sure that the meaning of each sentence was clear. Sometimes Black Elk sang the sacred songs and beat a drum, as in the old way. On many days other old friends joined Black Elk, and the talks would go on after supper, late into the night. There was so much to tell.

Black Elk's Pipe

Black Elk wanted to teach John Neihardt the meaning of the sacred traditions. Before he began talking, Black Elk filled his ceremonial pipe with red willow bark and offered it to the Spirit of the World, so that he might be sure to speak the truth.

The pipe had four ribbons hanging from its stem to represent the four quarters of the universe. Black Elk explained, "The black one is for the west, where the thunder beings live to send us rain; the white one for the north, whence comes the great white cleansing wind; the red one for the east, whence springs the light and where the Morning Star lives to give men wisdom; the yellow for the south, whence come the summer and the power to grow. But

Black Elk and Standing Bear shared with John
Neihardt many things sacred to their people,
including this drum and pipe.

these four spirits are only one Spirit after all, and the eagle feather
here is for that One, which is like a father." The bison hide wrapped
around the mouthpiece of the pipe was a reminder of the nourish-
ment given by Mother Earth.

Now It's Your Turn

MAKE A MORNING STAR

Black Elk said, "The Morning Star stands between the darkness and the light, and represents knowledge." It is also called the Daybreak Star. Did you ever hear people say that an idea just "dawned" on them? Is that what Black Elk meant?

You can make your own Morning Star to wear around your neck. With a grownup's help, cut two eight-pointed stars out of colored construction paper or felt, one about four inches wide and the other about two inches. You could use two shades of brown, to look like leather.

Glue the smaller star on top of the larger star. Attach a feather to the front or back of the Morning Star. If you don't have a real feather, cut out a feather shape from colored paper or felt. (Patterns for the star and feather can be found at the back of this book.) Thread a rawhide shoelace through two little holes in the center of the star, and knot the ends in the back. Now you can wear a Morning Star and let your thoughts rise as high as the eagle can fly.

A Traditional Feast

John Neihardt gave a feast for Black Elk's family and friends when the gathering of stories was almost done. Black Elk, the man of spirit, dressed in his best ceremonial clothing: beaded moccasins, trousers, a simple shirt decorated with porcupine quills, and a fur headpiece with a single eagle feather. The three hundred guests sat on the ground near the cabin in a large circle and waited patiently to be served by young men, who gave each person soup, meat, fruit pudding, bread, and hot coffee.

The Neihardts, Black Elk, and Chase-in-the-Morning are ready for the traditional hoop and spear game.

When the feast was over, Black Elk and Standing Bear performed an adoption and naming ceremony, officially taking the Neihardt family into the Oglala tribe. Black

Elk gave them holy names. Enid became She Who Walks with Her Holy Red Staff, to show that she would have a happy family life. The younger daughter, Hilda, was named Daybreak Star Woman, showing that she had a great desire for wisdom. And John Neihardt was honored with the name Flaming Rainbow. Hilda remembered Black Elk explaining, "The world is like a garden, and over this garden his words go like rain. Where they fall, they leave everything a little greener. And after his words have passed, the memory of them shall stand long in the west like a flaming rainbow."

Teaching Tales

Native Americans have always used storytelling as a way to teach sacred truths. Black Elk told many stories to his children and grandchildren. One of his favorites was about a competition among the birds to see who could fly longest up in the sky. All the birds flew up, and then one by one they fell back to earth as their wings became tired. Only the mighty eagle flew and flew and flew. Finally the eagle too came down and was named the winner.

But then someone saw a little tiny bird still flying around and around up in the sky. At last the little bird landed, and it was a hummingbird. "How did you do that? How did you stay up there so long?" asked the other birds. The little hummingbird replied, "Well, because I rode up on the back of the eagle."

Black Elk's story had two teachings for his listeners. First, it's good to use your mind—the little hummingbird figured out how to fly smarter, on the back of the eagle. And second, always tell the truth. The hummingbird didn't pretend that it had done all that flying by itself.

Black Elk and the Six Grandfathers

Black Elk wanted to once more visit the mountain peak where he had traveled in his spirit vision to meet the Six Grandfathers so many years earlier. The Neihardts drove with Black Elk and his son across the bare, treeless Badlands into the Black Hills of South Dakota, which are sacred to the Lakota. Then they hiked up to the special place on Harney Peak where visions have come to young warriors for centuries.

When they stopped on a flat rocky surface, Black Elk stood at the edge with his sacred pipe to send out his voice to the Six Grandfathers. He offered his pipe to the One Above. He prayed, "Grandfather, Great Spirit, once more behold me on earth and lean to hear my feeble voice. You lived first, and you are older than all need, older than all prayer. All things belong to you—the two-leggeds, the four-leggeds, the wings of the air, and all green things that live."

Black Elk prayed that the flowering tree at the center of the sacred hoop would grow again and be filled with singing birds. He ended his prayer to the Powers of the World with these words: "O make my people live!" By giving his living words to the poet Neihardt, Black Elk helped the tree to bloom again.

BUFFALO BILL'S
WILD WEST

An Amazing Life

John Neihardt gathered all the stories together into a book called *Black Elk Speaks*, which was first published in 1932. The book sold only a few hundred copies at that time, which was disappointing. However, the book continued to be admired and treasured by people around the world. It was published again in 1961. Then a popular television host interviewed John Neihardt about Black Elk, and suddenly Black Elk's book was in great demand.

Young people in the Native American communities learned the ways of their great-grandfathers from reading Black Elk's stories about his life. The spiritual beliefs and religion of the Plains Indians were preserved and passed on to new generations of Indian people. And many people of other faiths and traditions who read *Black Elk Speaks* learned to respect the Native American ways, as well. Isn't that amazing?

Fulfilling the Spirit Vision

Black Elk was an old man when he told his life story to John Neihardt. He lived for nearly twenty years more, continuing to teach and perform some of the ceremonies from his youth. He prayed every day—both the Catholic prayers he had learned when he was baptized on the reservation and the traditional Lakota prayers, as he offered his pipe to the One Spirit who loves and watches over all the children of the earth. And at the end of his very long life, Black Elk was grateful that he had been able to fulfill his vision of protecting his people's traditions, as the Great Spirit had told him he was meant to do.

The night after Black Elk died in 1950, the Northern Lights danced like fire in the sky over South Dakota.

Now It's Your Turn

NAMES THAT HAVE MEANING

In many cultures and religions, people are given special names to remind them of their spiritual qualities, or of their true natures, or of their accomplishments. Babies are blessed or baptized with a name, often in honor of a relative or a saint. Boys and girls earn nicknames for excelling in sports. People choose e-mail names to use on the Internet that show their interests or hobbies.

Black Elk gave the names Flaming Rainbow to John Neihardt and Daybreak Star Woman to Neihardt's daughter to share his vision with them. If Black Elk were to choose a special name for you, what might it be?

Think about your unique personality, your strengths, and your accomplishments. What name would show who you really are, or who you want to be? Might you be called He Who Always Walks with Friends? Or, Owl with Wise Eyes? Or, Dancing Feet Girl?

Ask your best friends to come up with a "Native American" name for you, too. Is it similar to the name you made up for yourself? How well do your friends know you?

Ask your family what your new name might be. But don't be mad if their name for you turns out to be something like Sleeps through the Alarm or Hides Peas under Plate!

Fascinating Fact

Black Elk and his friends went fishing in the sparkling river when they were young. The boys threw offerings of bait into the water and asked the fish to come to them. When they caught the first fish, they put it on a forked stick and kissed it. If they didn't kiss the fish, they believed, the other fish would stay away. If the first fish was too little, they kissed it and put it back, so it wouldn't scare off the bigger fish. Black Elk caught a lot of fish that way. But nowadays you shouldn't kiss a fish yourself!

Now It's Your Turn

CARING FOR MOTHER EARTH

One of the most important beliefs of Native Americans is that we must take care of Mother Earth. We must replace what we use and take only what we need. Then all living things will stay in balance.

In Black Elk's Oglala Lakota community, when people dig turnips from their gardens, they cut off the root of the turnip to eat and replace the top of the turnip, with its green leaves, in the hole. Another turnip will grow there. When they cut down a tree, they plant another in its place.

What can you do to help keep Mother Earth in balance? Perhaps your family or your class could plant a small tree to celebrate Earth Day or Arbor Day. You could ask to walk or ride your bike to an after-school practice, instead of using gasoline by riding in a car. Rather than throw the peels from fruit and vegetables into the garbage, maybe you could turn them into compost to feed a garden. Every little bit helps the earth.

Important Events in the Life of Black Elk

1872—Black Elk had a vision of Six Grandfathers, the Powers of the World, who gave him special gifts of healing, seeing, and teaching.

1876—He fought in the battle of the Little Bighorn at the age of thirteen, led by his cousin Crazy Horse.

1880—Black Elk told his vision to a medicine man, who created a Horse Dance ceremony to help him follow his spiritual path.

1887–1889—Black Elk traveled in Europe with Buffalo Bill's Wild West Show for nearly three years, becoming more and more homesick for his people and the plains.

1890—Black Elk witnessed the terrible massacre of the Sioux people at Wounded Knee by U.S. soldiers and feared that the sacred hoop of the world was breaking apart.

1904—Black Elk became a Roman Catholic, taking the saint's name Nicholas as his baptismal name.

1930—He met the writer John Neihardt and promised to tell him his life story in great detail the next spring. *Black Elk Speaks* was first published in 1932.

1950—Black Elk died of old age at home with his family.

Important Words to Know

Badlands—An area of South Dakota known for its gullies, steep ridges, and erosion of the land. Animals such as bison, bighorn sheep, antelope, and prairie dogs live in the Badlands.

Ghost Dance—A ritual dance that was done in the 1870s and 1880s by some Plains Indians who believed that a new land would be created to bring back the traditional and sacred way of life that had existed before the U.S. soldiers came. The tragic battle at Wounded Knee in 1890 ended the hopes of the Ghost Dance believers.

Medicine man—A man (or a woman) in a Native American community who heals the sick through the use of herbal medicine, prayer, and sacred ceremonies.

Reservations—Land that the U.S. government set aside for American Indians to live on. The Plains Indians were forced onto reservations during the late 1800s, when settlers spread west across the country. Today the tribes own and run the reservations.

Sacred Hoop—A Native American way to describe the way all life on earth is connected.

Sioux—The Native Americans of the Great Plains. The three main groups of the Sioux nation—Lakota, Nakota, and Dakota—were each made up of smaller tribes such as the Oglala, the Hunkpapa, and the Blackfeet.

Six Grandfathers—In the Plains Indian religious tradition, these old men represent the Powers of the World: the North, the South, the East, the West, the Sky, and the Earth.

Black Elk: Native American Man of Spirit

2004 First Printing
© 2004 by SkyLight Paths Publishing

Library of Congress Cataloging-in-Publication Data
Shaw, Maura D.
Black Elk : native American man of spirit / Maura D. Shaw ; illustrations by Stephen Marchesi.
p. cm. — (Spiritual biographies for young people)
ISBN 1-59473-043-1 (hardcover)
1. Black Elk, 1863–1950. 2. Oglala Indians—Biography. 3. Oglala Indians—Religion. I. Marchesi, Stephen. II. Title. III. Series.
E99.O3B5563 2004
978.004'975243'0092—dc22   2004012131

Manufactured in Hong Kong

1 2 3 4 5 6 7 8 9 10
We are most grateful to Hilda Neihardt and her daughter Coralie Hughes for their kind assistance and for the invaluable information found in Hilda Neihardt's book *Black Elk and Flaming Rainbow: Personal Memories of the Lakota Holy Man and John Neihardt* and in the book that she compiled from interviews with Black Elk's two granddaughters and two great-grandsons, called *Black Elk Lives: Conversations with the Black Elk Family*, both published by the University of Nebraska Press. A special thank you to Shelly Angers for her help in creating the activities in this book.

Grateful acknowledgment is given for permission to reprint material from the following sources: photos on pages 5, 9, 10, 12, and 16 courtesy of John G. Neihardt Papers, c. 1858–1974, Western Historical Manuscript Collection–Columbia, Missouri; photo on page 3 courtesy of the National Anthropological Archives, INV 00506100. Some images © clipart.com or istockphoto.com. Every effort has been made to trace and acknowledge copyright holders of all material used in this book. The publisher apologizes for any errors or omissions that may remain and asks that such be brought to our attention for correction in future editions.

SkyLight Paths, "Walking Together, Finding the Way" and colophon are trademarks of LongHill Partners, Inc., registered in the U.S. Patent and Trademark Office.

Walking Together, Finding the Way
Published by SkyLight Paths Publishing
A Division of LongHill Partners, Inc.
Sunset Farm Offices, Route 4, P.O. Box 237
Woodstock, VT 05091
Tel: (802) 457-4000   Fax: (802) 457-4004
www.skylightpaths.com

[Feather Pattern]

Photocopy this
page and then cut
out the pattern.

[Star Pattern]

[Star Pattern]

Photocopy this
page and then cut
out the patterns.